From Dying
To
Flying

Releasing the Power of Hope

E–Mail: davidholdaway1@aol.com

Cover design by Graham Alder

ISBN 978-1-907929-11-3

Life Publications

To Jan
For thirty wonderful years of
Marriage and for many more

From Dying to Flying

Contents

Introduction   9

Understanding Hope   15

Without Hope You Die Inside   25

Suffering, Hope and Glory   33

Groans of Pain and Songs of Hope   39

Afraid to Hope   47

You Can't Have Faith without Hope   57

Without God and Without Hope   65

Releasing The Power of Hope   75

God Will Make A Way   83

From Dying to Flying   91

Reasons to Hope   105

Hope Again   121

From Dying to Flying

*No one whose hope is in God will
ever be put to shame*

Psalm 25:3

From Dying to Flying

Introduction

Thousands of books and countless sermons have been written and preached about faith but in comparison relatively few about hope. Yet as we shall see you cannot have faith without hope because *'faith is the substance of things hoped for,'* (Hebrews 11: 1). Some of the reasons for this lack of teaching about hope are because we don't really understand what hope is and how vital and powerful it is to a life that is worth living.

On a visit to the famous Menninger Clinic in Topeka, Kansas, which specializes in the treatment of psychiatric patients, pastor and author Bruce Larson asked the staff to identify the single most important ingredient in the treatment of the mentally disturbed. They were unanimous in singling out hope as the most important factor, but went on to confess they didn't really know how to dispense hope to a patient. It is a quality of the spirit, and thus an elusive gift. Yet they could tell right away when a patient turned the corner in treatment and for the first time believed that the future did not have to be the same as the troubled present.

Jerome Groopman is Professor of Medicine at Harvard Medical School and one of the world's leading researchers in cancer and AIDS. In his latest book, *The Anatomy of Hope: How People Prevail in the Face of Illness*, he states boldly, "Hope, I have come to believe, is as vital to our lives as the very oxygen that we breathe."

He admits that he was once cynical of claims that hope could affect a patient's physical and mental health but chronicles the gradual opening of his mind, an education that was both professional and personal. He writes, "I slammed the door on hope and closed off my mind to seriously considering it as a catalyst in the crucible of cure." Using medical case studies from his own career, he illustrates how doctors can rely too heavily on optimism or harsh reality in the face of a grave prognosis. He describes how he gradually learned to live in the middle ground, neither shielding patients from the truth nor allowing them to be overcome by fear and doubt. He says, "We are just beginning to appreciate hope's reach and have not defined its limits…I see hope as the very heart of healing."

Such sentiments and insights are seen quite dramatically in the life Brryan Jackson (yes he spells his name that way) . Brryan is an accomplished and outspoken advocate for the power of hope, faith and forgiveness and credits his Christian belief for his hopefulness and sense of purpose that has made him happy despite his harrowing story.

When he was just an eleven month old baby, his father entered his hospital room and injected a syringe of HIV-tainted blood into his tiny body. His dad was seeking revenge on Jackson's mother for having the baby which he didn't want her to have or pay child support for. But Brryan lived despite being constantly sick and in 1996 when he was near death he was diagnosed with AIDS. Doctors, however, were puzzled as to how he contracted the disease because he was not born with it and had not received any blood transfusions which could have given him the illness. That is when suspicion turned on his father who worked as a St Louis hospital lab technician drawing blood from patients. He had previously threatened to harm his son and the jury at his trial were told how he came to the hospital one day and persuaded Brryan's mother to go and get something to eat while he stayed with the baby. Prosecutors said he had a syringe filled with blood tucked inside his lab coat and waited until he was alone with the boy to inject him. He was found guilty of first degree assault and sentenced to life in prison. The judge said in passing sentence that he was in the same category as the worst war criminal for what he had done.

As he grew up Brryan's daily medication included dozens of pills and injections which caused him to lose most of his hearing and he was constantly ridiculed by his peers. Today he is an active twenty-year-old studying business and communications. With advances and improvements in AIDS treatment and his positive hope filled attitude, he is in general good health. He has also forgiven his father for what he did to him.

In 2009 as a young 17 year-old man Brryan started a non profit organisation helping those with HIV which he called, *Hope is Vital.*

This book is not just about human hope it is about the awesome power of hope when it is founded in God and His promises. In the following pages we will understand what such hope is and what it is not. How it operates and why it is so powerful. How love releases it and faith requires it.

From Dying to Flying

"I know the plans I have for you,"
declares the Lord, "plans to prosper
you and not to harm you, plans to
give you hope and a future."

Jeremiah 29:11

From Dying to Flying

Understanding Hope

There was a dear, elderly couple in one of the churches I pastored who told me a rather amusing story of a weekend they went on with a national holiday company. Their destination was the south coast of England and as part of the three day break they would be going on a mystery tour to a place of historical interest. They were very excited about this and had hoped it was somewhere special they had never been before. So they traveled almost 200 miles to their seaside hotel and the second day the mystery coach trip began. It wasn't long before they realised they were travelling on the same route they had taken the day before. Some four hours later they arrived to visit a castle and park grounds that was just two miles from where they lived. They spent five hours in the park they had been to many times before and then it was the long trek back to their hotel. They arrived tired and disappointed but at least saw the funny side. They had hoped for an exciting day but it was not to be.

Biblical hope is not a mystery tour based on wishful thinking. It is a confident expectation and trust in who God is and what He has said. It is the expectancy and anticipation of good things. It is the opposite of dread, which imagines something bad will happen, but looks instead for something good. It believes that everything is going to turn out well because God is in control and He makes all things work for the good of those who love Him, Romans 8:28. Note that Paul doesn't say all things *are* good but they work *for* good.

Confusion often arises as to what "hope" really is and one of the major reasons is because what many think hope is and what the Bible teaches are not the same. Take for instance the follow expressions,

* We must hope for the best but prepare for the worst.
* I hope our team will win the championship but it's not very likely.
* I hope to win the lottery but the odds are 14 million to one.
* I hope it will not rain today.
* I hope you enjoy this.

We use the word hope in so many different ways so no wonder its confusing The Catholic tradition even has a patron saint for hopeless causes, Saint Jude, whose aid can be sought when "all hope is lost and there is no hope."

The standard dictionary definitions of "hope" are to *feel* that something desired *may* happen. But the words *feel* and *may* are very vague and indefinite. It's at best being positive and at worst merely a wishy washy kind of unsure optimism. It's assuming that things will just work out even if you have no good reason to think that they will. It goes beyond reasonable enthusiasm and ends up in the realm of denial. It's like the story about the man falling from a 100-storey building. As he passed the 50th floor, he said to himself, "Well, so far, so good!"

The Hebrew and Greek words translated by the word "hope" mean an "indication of certainty," "a strong and confident expectation."

There are about a dozen different Hebrew words rendered as "hope" in the Old Testament. One of them is *tiqvah* which is trust in an unbreakable promise. It literally refers to a cord or attachment, something strengthened by being bound together, such as a rope with its many strands which endures when tested and stretched.

There are only two Greek words for hope in the New Testament – *elpis* is an expectation or confidence, and its verb form, *elpizo*, is the act of expecting or trusting.

Such hope is not an escape from reality and life's trials and problems. It faces them square on but knows that God is greater than anything we can ever face. Neither does it leave us idle or drifting but motivates and energises us. It changes how we see ourselves. We are pilgrims on a journey. This world is not our home and this life is not all there is. It changes what we value. It makes us heavenly focused rather than earthly minded. It affects what we do with our lives, talents, time and treasures.

The Christian life, when understood according to God's truth, is a magnificent obsession with an eternal hope, a hope that does not lead to an escapist attitude, but to the pursuit of life on a whole new dimension.

It gives joy and peace

> *Now may the God of **hope** fill you with all joy and peace in believing, that you may abound in **hope** by the power of the Holy Spirit.*
>
> Romans 15:13

It gives us protection

> *Behold, the eye of the Lord is on those who fear Him, On those who **hope** for His loving kindness.*
>
> Psalm 33:18

It gives us strength, courage, boldness

> *Be strong, and let your heart take courage, All you who **hope** in the Lord.*
>
> Psalm 31:24

It gives us comfort and confidence in the face of death

> *But we do not want you to be uninformed, brethren, about those who are asleep, that you may not grieve, as do the rest who have no **hope**.*
>
> 1 Thessalonians 4:13

It gives us confidence in ministry

> *For it is for this we labour and strive, because we have fixed our **hope** on the living God, who is the Saviour of all men, especially of believers.*
>
> 1 Timothy 4:10

We can't enjoy and experience the Kingdom of God with a hopeless, negative mindset because everything in God's kingdom is positive. Therefore Biblical hope is a powerful, spiritual force. To enjoy life we must maintain a godly, encouraging outlook because God, who is the source of life, wants positive things to happen to each of us.

By nature much of our thinking tends to be negative, we see the problems in the possibilities far more than the possibilities in the problems. To illustrate this I sometimes hold up a white handkerchief with a small black spot marked in the centre and ask a congregation what they can see. Most respond a "black spot," so I then ask how many can see a large white handkerchief? They get the point.

It's important to point out that Biblical hope is not some kind of "power of positive thinking" that tries to convince yourself and others that everything is wonderful when it clearly is not.

In 1952 the man who has been called the father of positive thinking, Norman Vincent Peale, published a book that became one of the most popular of the twentieth century. *The Power of Positive Thinking* has sold more than twenty million copies in 41 languages and has influenced not one but several generations both inside and outside the church.

Peale's thesis is not simply about having a positive attitude and optimistic outlook, but being able to channel a spiritual power through your thoughts. Peale spoke of this power residing in all of us and coming from God but the problem is in his understanding of God, Jesus and salvation.

In an interview with Phil Donahue on his TV show in 1984, Peale said,

> "It's not necessary to be born again. You have your way to God; I have mine. I found eternal peace in a Shinto shrine... I've been to the Shinto shrines, and God is everywhere." Donahue exclaimed, "But you are a Christian minister; you're supposed to tell me that Christ is the Way and the Truth and the Life, aren't you?" Peale replied,

"Christ is one of the ways! God is everywhere."
Peale told Donahue that when he got to "the
Pearly Gates", "St. Peter" would say, "I like
Phil Donahue; let him in!"[1]

Peale was also a very prominent freemason and served as Grand
Chaplain of the Grand Lodge of New York City and Imperial
Grand Chaplain of the Shrine. On September 30, 1991, he was
inducted into the Scottish Rite Hall of Honour, and his oil portrait
hangs in the House of the Washington D.C. Temple.

In an article that appeared in the *Masonic Scottish Rite Journal*
in February 1993, Peale said,

> "My grandfather was a Mason for 50 years,
> my father for 50 years, and I have been a
> Mason for over 60 years. This means my tie
> with Freemasonry extends back to 1869 when
> my grandfather joined the Masons."

It is not the power of positive thinking but the power of godly
thinking which is positive that the Bible affirms. It is not about
having "hope in hope" or "faith in faith" but having our hope and
faith rooted in Jesus Christ.

Such hope and faith makes us happy, optimistic and full of
strength and courage and because it is such a powerful force, the
devil goes after it with a vengeance. If he can steal our hope, he
will undermine our faith and set us on a path toward depression
and despair.

There's something about hope that makes people lighthearted
and joyful. It's fun and encouraging to be around them. Life just
seems to flow out of them. Where as those without hope tend to
drain the life from you. A pessimist has been described as a

person who is always building dungeons in the air and if we are not careful we can end up in there with them.

When we have true hope our outlook on life is positive and we trust in God's love. It keeps us from worry and anxiety and empowers us to remain in God's peace. It helps us look forward to what's ahead with excitement and confidence. You're not going to be happy if you don't have hope. The more hope you have in God, the happier you become.

When you think about the future, are you hopeful? Are you insistently hoping for something good to happen to you? Do you wake up in the morning excited and expectant about life? Do you say, "Good morning Lord" or "Good Lord, it's morning!"?

1 Hugh Pyle, *Sword of the Lord*, December 14 1984

From Dying to Flying

Take from a man his wealth, and you hinder him; take from him his purpose, and you slow him down. But take from man his hope, and you stop him. He can go on without wealth, and even without purpose, for awhile. But he will not go on without hope.

C. Neil Strait

From Dying to Flying

Without Hope You Die Inside

In his book *Hope Can Make You Well* Norman Cousins, a prolific author and professor of Medical Humanities at the University of California, tells of a 17-year-old young man who had undergone brain surgery in a Los Angeles hospital. His father, who was a doctor, was sitting by his bedside when the surgeon came in and apologetically explained to him that he hadn't been able to remove the entire tumour, it was embedded too deeply. He told the father that his son probably only had a week to ten days to live.

Suddenly the father heard sobbing coming from his son's bed. He turned around and realized that he was conscious and had heard what the surgeon said. The dad put his hand on the young man's shoulder and said, "Listen, son, I don't accept what he says, and you shouldn't either. I've seen too many cases where people who were supposed to die came through. You've got to believe me. No doctor really knows enough to make that kind of prediction."

Instead of fear and despair taking hold of his son, the father spoke life and the young man began to hope. Six years later he was still in remission and doing well. His attitude of hope was a major factor in his remarkable recovery. 2

Doctors do know what they are talking about (most of the time) as do Pastors (again most of the time). Only God, however, is God and though we must give the facts as we see them we must be careful not to destroy hope in the process, otherwise the spiritual and emotional damage becomes as devastating as the prognosis.

"What oxygen is to the lungs," observed the Swiss theologian Emil Brunner, "such is hope for the meaning of life." We can struggle for a time gasping and panting for every breath we draw but sooner or later the sheer effort to survive becomes overwhelming and we either give up on any truly meaningful purpose or on life itself.

Dr S. I. McMillen discusses how the power of hope affects our health in his classic book *None of These Diseases* which has sold more than one million copies. He tells of how in the 1940s, more than thirty-one thousand allied soldiers were detained as prisoners in Japan and Korea. Later studies of these soldiers showed that more died from a lack of hope than anything else. Quoting Dr Harold Wolff, "Many died from despair. Hope, like faith is a purpose in life, is medicinal. This is not really a statement of belief, but a conclusion proved by meticulously controlled scientific experiment."3

Contrast the following two outlooks on life. One is by the movie producer Woody Allen and the other the famous evangelist Billy Graham. Allen once gave the commencement address at Yale University. He said, "Our civilization stands at the crossroads. Down one road is despondency and despair. Down the other road is total annihilation. I hope we'll take the right road."

Without Hope You Die Inside

Obviously he was trying to be funny, but his statement reflects his own battles with the depression and pessimism of our times. He once said, "My mother always said I was a very cheerful kid until I was 5 years old, and then I turned gloomy."

Graham, now 91, said, "Everywhere I go I find that people, both leaders and individuals, are asking one basic question, is there any hope for the future? My answer is yes, through Jesus Christ."

Without hope we die inside. The human spirit thrives on hope and the heart can withstand almost any trial or disappointment as long as the spirit sustains you. But when you lose hope you lose heart and it crushes the spirit making life unbearable.

This is vividly portrayed in Victor Hugo's famous novel *Les Miserables* (the wretched poor ones) which is a story of forgiveness and redemption, hope and despair set in nineteenth century France.

One of the most tragic characters in the book is a young, single mother, Fantine, who works in a factory to support her daughter, Cosette, whom she had to send away to live with an innkeeper. Fired for refusing the sexual advances of the foreman she finds herself on the streets without a job and unable to support her child. She has been pitilessly abandoned by her child's father and forced to sell her hair and some of her teeth to try and pay for her daughter's care.

In the musical of the story she sings one its most powerful and moving songs of a life that was once filled with hope and excitement about the future,

> *I had a dream in time gone by*
> *When hope was high*
> *And life worth living,*

I dreamed that love would never die,
I dreamed that God would be forgiving.

She is remembering the time when she was young and unafraid. She sings of a love filling her days with joy and endless wonder. "A time when hope was high and life worth living." She met a man she loved who became the father of her child and then left them and disappeared. Now abandoned and betrayed she ends by singing,

I had a dream that life would be
So different from this hell I'm living;
So different now from what it seemed
Now life has killed the dream I dreamed.

In one of the churches we pastored my wife Jan and I were asked to see a young woman in her early thirties who was struggling to bring up three young children and had become an alcoholic. She told us the harrowing story of her young life, how she had been deceived and taken advantage of by someone she trusted as a spiritual father figure. How she had been forced and humiliated into leaving her husband and running away to where she could not be found. As she shared our hearts ached for her. Now she was desperate. She was a Christian when all this had happened but felt deeply ashamed how she had failed God and her family. Her life had spiraled out of control and drink was her solace and tormentor.

As we talked and prayed with her it was obvious she hated herself and her life and could see no way forward. We assured her how much God still loved her and led her in prayer asking Him to forgive and heal her. After we prayed I said, "Only God has the power to forgive sins but if you truly meant what you just told Him then you need to hear these words, 'You are forgiven.'"

She started to cry but these were tears of life as a smile came over her face and a massive burden lifted from her. A new journey had begun. Hope had returned for the future.

"Hope deferred makes the heart sick,
but when the desire is fulfilled, it is a tree of life."

Proverbs 13:12.

2 *Hope Can Make You Well*, Norman Cousins. Parade, Oct 29, 1989.
3 *A Scientific Report on What Hope Does for Man*. S. I. Mcmillen, M.D., *None of These Diseases*. Reming H. Revell Co. Copyright 1968, p. ll0.

From Dying to Flying

We must accept finite disappointment, but never lose infinite hope.

Martin Luther King, Jr.

From Dying to Flying

Suffering, Hope and Glory

We can learn a lot from a caterpillar.

Admittedly they are not very pretty but once they break free from the cocoon of their old nature and become butterflies, the change is incredible. A creature that could only crawl can now soar. But such transformation requires a growth process.

The adult butterfly lays eggs which hatch out in about 3-7 days. The young caterpillars start off eating and hardly stop for two to three weeks. During this time their body mass will increase by a few thousand times developing up to 4000 muscles and six pairs of eyes.

When the caterpillar is ready to go through its metamorphosis it will find a place on a stem or branch and attach itself by spinning its own silk. About 24 hours later it will wiggle like crazy shedding its skeleton revealing the chrysalis beneath. Although it appears to be motionless, inside tremendous change is taking place. Its anatomy is being reconstructed into the adult butterfly which will emerge in about one to two weeks. At first it will be unable to fly. But as it strains to pump fluid from its body into its crumpled wings they begin to strengthen. After several hours it will be able to fly.

You may have read or heard the story of the young boy who found a caterpillar and took it home to see what would happen to it. One day the insect climbed up a stick and started creating a cocoon. The little boy was thrilled to see the changes and watched every day, waiting for the butterfly to emerge. One day it happened, a small hole appeared in the cocoon and the butterfly started its struggle to emerge. Excitement soon turned to frustration and concern. The butterfly was struggling so hard to get out! It looked as if it couldn't break free! So the boy decided to help. With a pair of scissors he snipped the cocoon to make the hole bigger and soon the butterfly emerged! But something was wrong.

It had a swollen body and small, shriveled wings. This meant that for the rest of its short life it crawled around with a bloated body and crippled wings. It would never be able to fly. What the child didn't realise was that the butterfly's struggle to push its way through the tiny opening of the cocoon pushed the fluid out of its body and into its wings. Without the struggle, the butterfly could not fly.

One of the strengths of having a pastoral gifting is that of being able to empathize and care for others, but over the years I have discovered it can have a very subtle danger attached to it. When someone is in need or going through trials the desire is to resolve the problems, heal the pain and ease the struggle immediately. However, there are times when God is at work in the process and we can sometimes, by seeking to help, be getting in His way. We need wisdom as well as compassion for there can be a purpose to the struggle we do not see or understand. In the words of a famous Andrae Crouch song, "If we never had a problem, we'd never know God could solve them, never know what faith in His Word could do." It is often in the cocoon or the crucible that our character and trust in God is formed. We could never be overcomers unless there were things for us to overcome. It is only when we feel the stress of the storm that we learn the strength of the anchor.

Why there is so much suffering is a huge moral and theological issue. Something has gone terribly wrong in our world and it is not how God created or intended it. Sin and Satan have brought a terrible curse. The good news is that Jesus took our punishment and suffering upon Himself at the cross and there is coming a time when God will put an end to it all, there will be no more pain, death or tears, Revelation 21:4. In the meantime suffering is there to show us when things have gone wrong or to make us strong. It can either drive us from God or to Him. It can make us bitter or better. It can focus us on what is truly important in life or cause us to give up on life altogether. What makes the difference is our attitude and understanding of the cross.

Those who have trusted in God through hard times become people of depth in their relationship with God. Recently, a wonderful friend of mine died of Leukaemia. He was 94 years of age and until the final few months had led a full and active life. He had known a fair share of trials and suffering. When in his forties his first wife died of cancer and he was left to bring up three teenage boys. He told me on one occasion when in his mid eighties, that there were times in his life when he didn't understand why things happened and the pressures and heartache felt too great but added, "Yet at those times we can always come to the cross."

The words suffering, hope and glory are frequent themes mentioned together in Scripture. It is the power of hope which becomes the bridge between experiencing the suffering and encountering the glory.

> *I consider that our present sufferings are not worth comparing with the glory that will be revealed in us.*
>
> Romans 8:18

Faith goes up the stairs that love has made and looks out of the windows which hope has opened.

C H Spurgeon

From Dying to Flying

Groans of Pain and Songs of Hope

I love the story of the midwife who, walking through a hospital ward, heard the loud groans of a man whose dislocated shoulder was being reset. She walked over to his bed afterwards and said, "I've just come from the maternity ward and delivered a 10 pound baby and his mother didn't make half the fuss you are making." The patient grimaced back at her and said, "Try putting it back."

It's amazing how much suffering we are able to endure when we know there is a purpose and the end result is worth it.

Charles Haddon Spurgeon was one of the nineteenth century's greatest preachers. He regularly drew to his services government ministers and members of the royal family. When he arrived at The New Park Street Church in London, in 1854, the congregation had 232 members. By the end of his pastorate, 38 years later, that number had increased to 5,311, which was the largest independent congregation in the world. During his lifetime it is estimated he preached to more than ten million people. (Remember there was no radio or television).

But this only reveals a part of his life and ministry. He also suffered black periods of tormenting depression. One Sunday morning in 1866, he shocked his five thousand listeners when he announced, "I am the subject of depressions of spirit so fearful that I hope none of you ever gets to such extremes of wretchedness as I go to."

His wife, Susannah, became an invalid at age 33. He suffered terribly with a joint disorder that was diagnosed as gout. He was forced to stay in bed, sometimes for weeks at a time in excruciating pain. "I have been brought very low," he wrote to his congregation during one long bout. "My flesh has been tortured with pain and my spirit has been prostrate with depression… With some difficulty I write these lines in my bed, mingling them with the groans of pain and the songs of hope."

In some medical journals it is reported that more human suffering has resulted from depression than any other single illness affecting mankind. That is a big statement but depression is a big problem and those who have suffered from it will tell you it can be worse than anything else they have experienced. The reason is that it can be not only physical but emotional, spiritual and psychological. It can affect every aspect of the human condition.

Depression is more common and complicated than many realise. Over three million people are affected by it each year in the UK alone. It is the number one psychological disorder in the western world. It is growing in all age groups, in virtually every community, and the growth is seen most in the young, especially teens. At this rate of increase, it will be the second most disabling condition in the world by 2020, behind heart disease. It also has many different causes and cures.

It can be caused by a sinful lifestyle, or the stress of overwork, or by a sudden tragedy or inherited tendencies to be anxious and melancholy. There are also many different cures. For some it is simply a change of scenery, but for others it needs a complete change of lifestyle. Some need little more than friendship and wise counsel while others need medical help and support.

Having experienced the anguish of depression myself I often share with those going through it that what they are experiencing will pass. I also reassure those severely depressed, they are not losing their mind. The fear and anxiety is normal for what is happening within the chemical processes and reactions in the body. Sadly, Christians often deal with depression far worse than others. They can live under the added guilt of thinking they are failing in their testimony because didn't Jesus say, *"I have come that you might have life in all its fullness,"* John 10:10, and, *"The fruit of the Spirit is joy,"* Galatians 5:22? They are then afraid to admit their condition and get the help they need. Why is it that you may have no problem going to the doctors and taking antibiotics for an infection but are reluctant to take anti depressants when they would be helpful? If you need antibiotics take them and if you need anti depressants take them. If you are worried about them being addictive speak to the doctor. There are many types that are not.

I also encourage those battling depression to read Psalms 42 and 43 which declare and release the power of hope. These two Psalms are one in the original Hebrew and as the Psalmist acknowledges his emotional pain and mental anguish three times he speaks to himself and says,

> *Why are you downcast, O my soul? Why so*
> *disturbed within me? Put your hope in God,*

*for I will yet praise him, my Saviour and
my God.*

Psalm 42:5,11, 43:5

If you don't speak to your emotions and troubles they will keep speaking to you. Jesus said if we speak to the mountain it will be cast into the sea, Mark 11:23. He uses the example of a mountain because if that can be moved anything can. But He is saying there is not only a time to talk to God about how big our problems are but also to talk to our problems and needs and tell them how big our God is. The Psalmist tells God about what's happening within his soul but ends with telling his soul to put its hope in God.

Rhythm and blues singer Robert Sylvester Kelly has had his share of life's groans of pain and songs of hope. His most famous song, *I Believe I Can Fly*, won him three Grammy Awards and was featured on the sound track of the film *Space Jam*. I heard an intriguing account of how he came to write it.

He phoned his sister to say he was going to end his life, he couldn't go on. She persuaded him to attend a church service with her and at the end of the meeting he went to the front to speak to the preacher telling him his life was in a mess and he needed help. He said that he couldn't go on living and saw no reason to do so. The minister told him that it didn't have to be that way and used the phrase, "If you can see it you can do it." Kelly told him, "I understand."

Not long after Michael Jordan, the American basketball star, phoned him to say he needed a theme song for a new film and asked if he would write it. Kelly agreed as he was not doing anything else and from his pain came a song of hope,

Groans of Pain and Songs of Hope

I used to think that I could not go on, And life was nothing but
an awful song, But now I know the meaning of true love, I'm
leaning on the everlasting arms,

If I can see it, then I can do it
If I just believe it, there's nothing to it.

I believe I can fly,
I believe I can touch the sky.
I think about it every night and day
Spread my wings and fly away.
I believe I can soar,
I see me running through an open door.
I believe I can fly, I believe I can fly,
I believe I can fly.

See I was on the verge of breakin' down,
Sometimes silence can seem so loud,
There are miracles in life I must achieve,
But first I know it starts inside of me.

,If I can see it then I can be it.
If I just believe it, there's nothing to it,

I believe I can fly...

The American preacher and writer Chuck Swindoll tells the story
of a lady who, while vacuuming her birdcage, was distracted for
a moment and sucked her budgie into the cleaner. Seeing the
empty cage she quickly emptied the bag of dust and fluff but little
Joey was barely alive. She plunged him under a cold water tap
and managed to freeze him in the process. As she heard his little
beak chattering and realised she was doing more harm than good

she rushed to get her hair dryer and blasted little Joey with red hot air, almost cooking him alive. Somehow Joey managed to survive but only just. Swindoll finished by saying, "Little Joey doesn't sing much anymore."

Life can be tough but make sure it doesn't steal your song.

Blessed is the man who expects nothing, for he shall never be disappointed.

Alexander Pope

From Dying to Flying

Afraid To Hope

Let's face it, there is a lot of hype about – even in the church. Unlike the fire that came down from heaven on Mount Carmel there is an awful lot that is worked up from below in many church services. "Everyone here is going to be healed!" "You are going to be rich!" "All your problems will be over!" Often it is well meaning but it can still do more harm than good. Sometimes it's simply the excitement and enthusiasm of the moment but it can also be manipulation and the ramblings of a skewed theology.

In 1 Samuel 4 we read the Israelites took the Ark of the Covenant into battle against the Philistines. God's people were now treating the symbol of His presence like a lucky charm, an eleventh century BC promise box which they believed would cause them to triumph over their enemies. Religious superstition had replaced relationship and spirituality. They thought that as long as they took the golden container with them and screamed loud and long enough, victory would be theirs.

But they had hardened their hearts and lived as they

pleased and God would not be used however much they sang and shouted.

While faith is the substance of things hoped for frustration is the substance of things hyped for. When you have been on the wrong end of hype enough times it leaves deep scars on your faith and the accumulated debris of disappointments and confused expectation can make you afraid to hope. It's much simpler and less of a roller coaster to live at a low level of expectancy and hide in the sovereignty of God. Don't get me wrong, there is great rest in God's sovereignty but it's not there to make us apathetic and fatalistic and develop a "whatever will be will be" attitude. Rather it's "what He wants to be will be." We are to pray *"thy Kingdom come, Thy will be done on earth as it is in heaven."*

It's not only public hype but our private hurts that can cause us to be afraid to hope. Take prayer for instance – it's wonderfully comforting but can also be frustratingly confusing. There are few things as exciting as having our prayers answered the way we expected. Wow! God is taking care of us. But equally, we wonder what is happening when they don't get answered for what we ask. This is one of the main reasons Christians find it difficult to pray. Prayer meetings are always one of the lowest attended church services.

The confusion comes because we believe we are praying to an awesome all powerful and loving God and yet we asked for healing and the person died. We are praying for a new job and all we have had are rejection letters. We were convinced God wanted to open the "door" but it's been shut in our face. So we develop a love hate relationship with prayer. We love the presence of God, the amazing answers it brings, but hate the disappointments and confusion.

I love the honesty of the late Ruth Graham (married to the evangelist Billy Graham) who said, "God has not always answered my prayers. If He had, I would have married the wrong man – several times."

Answers to Prayer

There are four different ways God can respond to our requests. It can be yes, no or wait (delays are not denials). There are also times when God answers but works it out in a different way – it's the same outcome to what we wanted. We travel down a different road but arrive at the same destination.

When Paul asked the believers in Rome to pray that he would be able to visit them in Rome, (Romans 15:31,32), their prayer was answered but I am sure not in the way any of them expected. After two long years he finally arrived, but as a prisoner under house arrest. However during that first imprisonment he wrote four New Testament books, Ephesians, Philippians, Colossians and Philemon.

In his book *Legacy of Sovereign Joy*, John Piper writes about the conversion of Augustine who was to become one of the great leaders of the church,

> At the age of 16 in the year 371, Augustine sneaked away from his mother in Carthage. During the night he sailed away to Rome, leaving her alone to her tears and her prayers.
>
> How were these prayers answered? Not the way Monica [Augustine's mother] hoped at the time. Only later could she see that praying is the deepest path to joy.

Augustine himself wrote, "And what did she beg of you, my God, with all those tears, if not that you would prevent me from sailing? But you did not do as she asked you. Instead, in the depth of your wisdom, you granted the wish that was closest to her heart.

"For she saw that you had granted her far more than she used to ask in her tearful prayers. You converted me to yourself, so that I no longer placed any hope in this world, but stood firmly upon the rule of faith. And you turned her sadness into rejoicing, into joy far fuller than her dearest wish, far sweeter and more chaste than any she had hoped to find."

When Amy Carmichael left Northern Ireland to serve God as a missionary in Japan in 1891, she was just 24 years of age. A year later after suffering ill health and receiving medical attention, she worked briefly in China and after a short furlough at home, she set sail for India where she worked and ministered without a furlough for the next 55 years until her death.

As a young girl she often prayed for God to change the colour of her brown eyes to blue. But years later realized that her brown eyes made her far more acceptable in Indian culture.

In 1901 she established the famous Dohnavur Fellowship and orphanage rescuing young girls from being sacrificed to Hindu gods or sold as sex slaves into the temples. Again her brown eyes were essential as dressed in Indian clothes she infiltrated the temples to rescue the girls. Blue eyes would have given her away. As we grow as Christians God wants us to develop a deeper relationship with Him. Prayer becomes more getting to know Him than getting what we want. He desires to give us first more of Himself and not just from Himself.

While we must guard against hype which is just fanciful hope we must also watch out for the other imposter which is having only a "forlorn hope." This is when we sigh in despair and say, "All we can do now is just hope."

The origin of the term "forlorn hope" comes from a Dutch word meaning a "lost troop." It refers to the first wave of soldiers who attack a breach in heavily defended positions. Those first in would face the full ferocity of gunfire and cannon and few if any survived. The dictionary describes it as a hopeless and desperate enterprise.

Some are afraid to hope because they have experienced so much hurt and disillusionment that they don't think they can face any more pain or disappointment. They simply or subconsciously refuse to hope so they won't be let down and discouraged. However understandable this might be it sets up a negative lifestyle. Everything becomes downbeat and pessimistic. They are like the person who says, "I always feel bad when I feel good in case I feel bad tomorrow."

It's Time To Hope Again

Jesus promised, *"Anyone who receives a prophet because he is a prophet will receive a prophet's reward,"* Matthew 10:41.

There was a woman in the Old Testament who experienced this long before Jesus said it. She lived in the small village of Shunem and had a wonderful gift of hospitality providing a room in her home for the prophet Elisha any time he wanted to use it. One day, the prophet asked if he could reward her in some way (2 Kings 4). She replied she had all she wanted but then Elisha's servant told him that she was without a child and that her husband was old. So the prophet promised her that in one year's time she would be holding a baby boy in her arms. Listen to her anguished reply, *"'No, my lord,' she objected. 'Don't mislead your servant, O man of God!'"* 2 Kings 4:16. It's the reaction that says, I can't bear any more disappointments and false hopes. She had probably prayed for many years for the son she longed for and month after month her hopes would bring frustration and despair. She still revered God and His servants and had heard of the miracles Elisha had done so she had not stopped believing in the miraculous, but it was for others and not for her.

I can understand a little of what she went through because when my wife and I were hoping for a child we knew the anguish and fear of months and years passing and facing the possibility we couldn't have children. Finally we did, and we refer to our daughter as "God's miracle." My wife and I were in a service listening to a message about the axe head that floated (2 Kings 6:6,7). The preacher said, "It is time to believe God and grab your miracle!" These were anointed words and God's presence filled the auditorium and so, along with hundreds of others, we stood before the Lord to take hold of the miracle we needed. I noticed my wife, Jan, swaying under the power of the Holy Spirit. God was in this moment and our hope was in Him. Almost a year later our daughter was born.

Afraid to Hope

When Elisha told the Shummanite her first reaction was "don't raise my hopes," but something was birthed in her spirit before a child was birthed in her womb. She went and lay with her elderly husband and as promised she conceived her miracle.

When hope is fading or has died we need to get into the presence of God and hear His Word. I know there will be those of you who, like myself, have received "prophetic words" which have proved to be more well meaning than true. But don't close your spirit to the prophetic. Just because some have got it wrong or the timing has not worked out it doesn't mean that God has forgotten you and your dreams will never come to pass.

Here is the poem that Amy Carmichael wrote to keep her hope in God undiminished and her desire to serve Him burning.

> Give me the Love that leads the way,
> The Faith that nothing can dismay,
> The Hope no disappointments tire,
> The Passion that'll burn like fire,
> Let me not sink to be a clod,
> Make me Thy fuel, Flame of God

From Dying to Flying

Hope is hearing the music of the future
Faith is dancing to it today.

From Dying to Flying

You Can't Have Faith Without Hope

A story is told of a church at a time of great crisis. A special meeting was called and opened with prayer by the chairman. He addressed God as "Almighty and eternal God, whose power is greater than all and whose grace is sufficient for us in every circumstance." When he finished, the business part of the meeting began and he introduced it by saying, "Ladies and gentlemen the situation we face is completely hopeless."

It's amazing how much we say we believe but then times of difficulty, fear and unbelief rob us of our faith and hope. When trials come some people go to peace while others go to pieces. It depends where our heart and minds are set. It isn't only about what we face but how we face it.

As I mentioned earlier so much has been spoken and written about faith and comparatively little about hope but you can't have faith without hope. Biblical faith is a close relative of hope – you cannot have one without the other because hope is the foundation on which faith builds. If we have no hope then faith has no where to stand. This is why we are told, *"Now faith is being sure of what we hope for and certain of what we do not see,"* Hebrews 11:1.

The devil attacks our hope to destroy our faith. We are not overcome by what comes against us or goes on around us. It's what happens within us that determines our trust in God and with it our peace and joy. We are never beaten until we are defeated on the inside and this only happens when we lose hope, it's then we want to give in and give up.

This is the reason the devil is always trying to put thoughts of dread and despair into our minds. He says, "You won't get well – you will die of that sickness." "You will never find anyone to love you," "You will always be in debt." "The depression will never leave." "God will not forgive you." And so the list goes on. It's all for the same purpose – to make us feel confused about God's love and lose hope. This is why we are told to put on, *"The helmet, the hope of salvation,"* 1 Thessalonians 5:8.

Hope sees the bigger picture when circumstances try to get us despairing and confused in the detail. It understands that the truth is even more powerful than the facts. The fact maybe that naturally the situation, the sickness, the prognosis is hopeless but the truth is that Jesus is the healer and will always have the final word in our lives. I heard a powerful quote recently which was printed on a postcard, it read, "It's going to be ok in the end so if it's not ok it's not the end."

But what about the times when people have been told to have hope for their healing and miracle and it didn't happen? It's one of the most difficult and painful issues we face, especially when it happens to loved ones and friends.

At the end of a talk I once gave about the ways God answers prayer a lady approached me and asked how she should pray for a close friend who was dying with cancer. She said, "I want to pray positively because I know God heals, but I also know people who were told they would be healed and died and their family and church were left confused and devastated." I told her I always encourage people to pray in hope and faith in such circumstances but also with wisdom. I shared that God's will (the big picture) is that His kingdom comes on earth as it is in heaven and healing is a part of His kingdom. I also explained that the fullness of His kingdom will only come when Jesus returns so we live in the tension of not knowing or being able to understand all the details of how and when and why. But we must start with what do know otherwise hope and faith will have nothing to be founded upon. I said we should always pray with and minister hope for healing unless we receive a clear word from God to pray for something else. I told her about the Apostle Paul asking three times to be freed from his thorn in the flesh. Paul must have hoped for and expected a response because he kept asking until one came. God eventually said His grace would be sufficient and that was enough for Paul. So either God takes it away or He empowers us so that those things have no power over us. That seemed to help her, I know it helps me.

Biblical hope is not the same as presumption. Hope is knowing that God loves us and is in complete control. Presumption is assuming we know exactly how everything should be. We must be so careful not to presume because often it is our pride or good intentions directing us.

Only God has all the answers and Jesus will always have the last word so we must not let the mystery deprive us of the reality, nor let what we do not know rob us of the hope for what we do know.

The Power of Hope versus the Power of Dread

You cannot manufacture faith and work it up. It comes from walking with God, and by hearing His word, (Romans 10:17). So when confronted by trials or sickness and you find it hard to have faith – ask God for hope. Focus on Him and not the problems and faith will come. When Jesus says faith as small as a mustard seed can cause mountains to be cast into the sea, He is telling us that if they can be removed anything can. The great "healing evangelist" Kathryn Kuhlman said, "The least amount of faith is mightier than the largest amount of power of the devil."

Jesus is also saying that it's not just the size of our faith but where it is founded and focused that is important, (*"have faith in God,"* Mark 11:22). Mountains may be huge but even the largest can be swallowed out of sight by the sea. It is still there but hidden by the depths of the waters. The same is true with whatever we face. It's not that we deny its reality but simply its right to dominate our vision and have power over our life. By the power of hope and faith in God we can not only call those things that are not as if they are (Romans 4:17-21) but also declare those things that are as if they are not. They are there but, like the mountain, are in the ocean swallowed up in the love and power of God. Compared to us the mountains are huge, but compared to God they are tiny.

When you read the Psalms it is striking how often they speak of hope in desperate situations. The Psalmist's hope is always first in God and then in His deliverance. Likewise, our hope must also first be in God and then His healing and provision. The Lord is our provider but first He is Jehovah and then Jireh – the God who provides.

Wherever Jesus went He brought hope. A leper says, *"If you are willing, you can make me clean,"* and Jesus answers, *"I am willing, be clean,"* Mark 1:40, 41. A blind man, a sick woman, a grieving family, a poor little rich man – the list is endless. When they hear Jesus is in town they begin to hope and faith starts to rise.

From Dying to Flying

*In Christ we have been saved
from 'a hopeless end' to
'an endless hope.'*

From Dying to Flying

Without God and Without Hope

Mr Herbert Norman, the Canadian Ambassador to Egypt, committed suicide yesterday by jumping from the top floor of a block of flats to the street below, announced the *Egyptian Gazette* on its front page on Friday, April 5, 1957. The newspaper told how, after asking Costa, his chauffeur, to wait for him "Mr Norman left his house at 9.30am and walked to the building where the Swedish Minister, Mr Brynolf Eng, lives. He took the lift to the eighth floor, walked up a few steps to the roof of the building, and jumped."

There was a note to his wife found in his jacket pocket which read, "My darling I have no option. I must kill myself, because I cannot live without hope."

Herbert Norman was a brilliant historian and diplomat with what it seemed so much to live with but tragically to him so little to live for.

In his book *Hope, Respect, Trust*, Joel Edwards, the former president of the Evangelical Alliance in the UK, relates a story detailing what happens when a culture loses hope. He says, "In

January 2003 I attended a 'gun summit' convened by the Home Secretary after the brutal murder of two young women in Aston, Birmingham. During the meeting a senior police officer made a memorable statement, 'What we need are exit routes from the hopelessness facing our young people.' Not long after that I met with the chief of police in the West Midlands. When I asked for an explanation on why young people shot each other in order to gain respect, his answer was quite simple, 'A lack of hope.'"

Toward the end of his life, British novelist and atheist H G Wells grew increasingly despairing about the fate of the human race. He said mankind had failed because evolution had failed to produce in us the right kind of brain. Therefore, we will destroy ourselves, die out as a species, and revert to the mud and slime from which we arose and we shall deserve our fate.

He did not always feel that way and in 1914 said that World War I would be the war that would end all war, "This, the greatest of all wars, is not just another war. It is the last war."

But his optimism evaporated in the cauldron of life and world events. On his 65th birthday he said, "I am lonely and have never found peace."

After the horrors of World War II he wrote his last book which he called, *A Mind at the End of its Tether* , published shortly before his death in 1946. It was his vision of the future as a nightmare of hopelessness and despair. He wrote, "There is no way out, or round or through."

He is not the only prominent atheist to express his despair for the world. The philosopher Bertrand Russell, whose books included, *Why I Am Not A Christian,* wrote of his beliefs and of what was to come in his work, *A Free Man's Worship,*

> All the labour of the ages, all the devotion, all
> the inspiration, all the noon day brightness
> of human genius, are destined to extinction
> in the vast death of the solar system...the
> whole temple of man's achievement must
> inevitably be buried beneath the debris of a
> universe in ruins. Only within the
> scaffolding of these truths on the firm
> foundation of unyielding despair, can the
> soul's habitation henceforth be safely built.

His conclusion that our firm foundation can only be safely built on unyielding despair sounds like the nonsense it is and only inspires you to jump off the nearest bridge.

I understand why atheists like Wells and Russell wrote of their despair and anguish, because to be without God is ultimately to be without hope. The sign above the entrance to Dante's hell says, "Abandon hope all you who enter here."

Contrast the above statements with those of the great Methodist missionary and theologian, Eli Stanley Jones. His world view is filled with hope. In his 1942 devotional *Abundant Living* he writes,

> The early Christians did not say in dismay,
> "Look what the world has come to," but in
> delight they said, "Look what has come to the
> world." They saw not merely the ruin, but the
> resource for the reconstruction of that ruin.
> They saw not merely that sin did abound, but
> that grace did much more abound. On that
> assurance the pivot of history swung from
> blank despair, loss of moral nerve, and
> fatalism, to faith and confidence that at last
> sin had met its match.

Three months before the Hollywood star Steve McQueen discovered he had lung cancer he became a Christian. He had begun to take stock of his life and was looking for answers.

In a private meeting with the evangelist Billy Graham, McQueen spoke of his spiritual search and faith in Christ, but he also had many questions about the Bible and how he could be sure of eternal life. Graham turned his Bible to Titus 1:2 which read, *"In hope of eternal life, which God, who cannot lie, promised before the world began..."* That was the verse he had longed to hear. McQueen was excited and asked, "What was that verse again?" and told Graham he needed a pencil and some paper so he could write down the verse. Billy Graham instead gave him his Bible.

In the book, *Steve McQueen: A Tribute to the King of Cool*, Marshall Terrill relates the passing of the superstar when all the treatments failed and he ultimately died after developing an embolism. Terrill says he died "painlessly and quietly." Immediately after he died, his son Chad said he wanted to be alone with his father.

"Upon entering the room, Chad turned on the light...Steve's eyes were still open. Chad sat on the bed beside him. As he looked at Steve, he noticed something odd. His eyes, which had been gray the past six months, had returned to their bright blue colour. Chad also noticed the Bible that the Reverend Billy Graham had given to Steve. It now rested on his chest, opened to Steve's favourite verse, John 3:16. *'For God so loved the world that he gave his only begotten son, that whosoever believeth in him should not perish, but have everlasting life.'"*

McQueen had told the doctors, "You mentioned earlier about finding a cure in my life. Well, that cure was finding the Lord in my life."

It's been said that more lies are told at funerals than anywhere else. Those who have lived their lives without God are eulogized as wonderful people who must be in a better place. But no matter what words are spoken if we live without Christ and die without Him we spend eternity without Him and that is not heaven but hell.

A little over a month before he died, the famous atheist Jean-Paul Sartre declared that he so strongly resisted feelings of despair that he would say to himself, "I know I shall die in hope." Then in profound sadness, he would add, "But hope needs a foundation."[4]

The following words are those of one of America's most famous orators, Robert Ingersoll, who was nicknamed "the great agnostic." They were spoken at the funeral of his beloved brother, Ebon. It is the eulogy of a man without hope.

> Life is a dark and barren valley between the cold ice clad peaks of two eternities. We strive sometimes to look beyond the darkness for the light. Sometimes we cry for help, but there comes back to us nothing but the echo of our own cry.

Even after a lifetime of attacking religion and belief in God Ingersoll tries to find something to hold on to when he concludes,

> But in the night of death, hope sees a star, and listening love can hear the rustle of a wing.

When asked what he meant when he spoke about hope he said his words were simply a spontaneous eruption of affection and admitted he did not know what eternity would bring.

When Ingersoll died suddenly the news of his death stunned his family. His body was kept at home for several days because his wife was reluctant to part with it. It was eventually removed for the sake of the family's health. At his funeral his wife and daughter despairingly clung to his decaying body, it was all they had. The scene at the crematorium, as described in the local newspaper, said it was enough to make the heart of anyone ache.

The same year another famous American died, Dwight L Moody. On December 22, 1899, Moody awoke to his last winter dawn. Having grown increasingly weak during the night, he began to speak in slow measured words. "Earth recedes, heaven opens before me!" His son, Will, who was nearby, hurried across the room to his father's side.

"Father, you are dreaming," he said. "No. This is no dream, Will," Moody said. "It is beautiful. It is like a trance. If this is death, there is no valley, this is bliss; this is glorious." For a short time he rallied and rose from his bed and walked to the window, then feeling faint, again was helped back into bed.

His daughter, Emma, began to pray for his recovery, but he said, "No, no Emma, God is calling me, and I must go, this is my coronation day. I have been looking forward to it." Then he went to be with his Lord.

The funeral service was triumphant. There was no despair. Many remembered the words the evangelist had spoken earlier that year in New York City, "Someday you will read in the papers that Moody is dead. Don't you believe a word of it. At that moment I shall be more alive than I am now."

Atheists like Bertrand Russell and H G Wells have their hope about death and eternity. It is a hope that there will be absolute nothingness and an end to all existence. They hope there is no God, no heaven or hell and no punishment for sin. Their hope is in their philosophy and understanding.

Christians have a hope that is in Christ and the fact that He came to this earth died on a cross and rose again from the grave. The evidence for this is overwhelming. It is a hope rooted in history, testimony, experiencing God's presence and power, personal transformation, and the Word of God. A hope that is not only inspiring but intelligent and reasonable.

One of the supreme tragedies of life is that you can have so much to live with and yet have so little to live for. To be without Christ is to be *"Without God and without hope,"* Ephesians 2:12,13.

4 Our Daily Bread, April 17, 1995

From Dying to Flying

A single sunbeam is enough to drive away many shadows.

Saint Francis of Assisi

From Dying to Flying

Receiving and Releasing Hope

In November 2005, *Forbes Magazine* declared after interviewing a number of sports experts that Roger Bannister's four minute mile was "the greatest athletic achievement" of all time. On a windy spring day, on May 6, 1954, during an athletic meeting at Oxford University, Bannister ran a mile in three minutes 59.4 seconds.

For many years it was widely believed to be impossible for a human to run a mile in under four minutes and that it was a physical barrier no athlete could break without causing significant damage to their health. It had also become a major psychological barrier as well. Many had come close but try as they did no one was able to run a sub four minute mile. It was as elusive as the pot of gold at the end of the rainbow, spoken of and dreamt about but unachievable.

Describing the psychological impact of the four minute barrier in an interview with *Forbes,* Bannister, related that, "The world record then was four minutes 1.4 seconds, held by Sweden's Gunder Haegg. It had been stuck there for nine years, since 1945. It didn't seem logical to me, however, as a physiologist / doctor, that if you could run a mile in four minutes, one and a bit seconds, you couldn't break four minutes. But it had become a mental as well as a physical barrier. In fact the Australian, John Landy, having ran four minutes, two seconds, three times, is reported to have commented, 'It's like a wall.'" Yet within three years, after Bannister's achievement, 16 other runners also broke the four minute mile.

So what happened to the barriers? When Bannister broke four minutes he released the power of hope in others that it could be done. Six weeks later, even John Landy, who had thought in impossible, followed suit with 3:58, breaking Bannister's record.

Hope, like despair, is contagious. This is what made Winston Churchill such a great war time leader. He understood the power of hope and the destructiveness of hopelessness. He said, "All the great things are simple, and many can be expressed in a single word: freedom, justice, honour, duty, mercy, hope." Amongst a thousand other quotable sayings he also said, "A pessimist sees the difficulty in every opportunity; while an optimist sees the opportunity in every difficulty." His speeches inspired a nation that stood alone against the might of Nazism, to hope and fight.

People who have experienced and know God's faithfulness tend to be very hopeful about the present and the future. They know a bad situation can turn into a wonderful testimony.

When the prophet Jeremiah walked among the ruins of Jerusalem after the Babylonian invasion had torn it apart he was heart broken by the devastation. He had warned this would happen and the people turned against him just as they had turned against God. Yet in the midst of his lamentations he recalls the faithfulness of God. It is an amazing place to find one of the most powerful and moving passages in the whole of the Old Testament.

> *Yet this I call to mind and therefore I have hope: Because of the Lord's great love we are not consumed, for his compassions never fail. They are new every morning; great is your faithfulness.*
>
> *I say to myself, "The Lord is my portion; therefore I will wait for him." The Lord is good to those whose hope is in him, to the one who seeks him.*

Lamentations 3:21-25

One of the great hymns of the church is taken directly from this passage, written by Thomas Obadiah Chisholm and first published in 1923, *Great is Thy Faithfulness* was his testimony as he looked back over his life. Lamentations 3:22-23 was one of his favorite scriptures. At age 75, he wrote these words,

> My income has not been large at any time due to impaired health in the earlier years which has followed me on until now. Although I must not fail to record here the unfailing faithfulness of a covenant-keeping God and that He has given me many wonderful displays of His providing care, for which I am filled with astonishing gratefulness.

Jeremiah had been told by God to purchase a field from his cousin because after 70 years of exile the people and his descendants would once more possess the land. This happened exactly the way God said it would through the prayers of Daniel (Chapter 9) and the ministry of Ezra.

The power of hope is received and released when we call to mind the faithfulness of God in the past, the goodness of God in the present and the promises of God for the future.

As we recall He is faithful we become faith filled even in the darkest times. You can prove this right now. Take a few moments to thank Jesus for what He has done for you. Bring to mind His faithfulness. It doesn't matter how big the problem is, God is bigger. Whatever you need – He is able. If God is for you who can be against you?

Recalling and declaring His faithfulness releases hope.

When Abraham and Sarah were in the twilight years of their life God said they would have a child. Humanly, it was impossible but Abraham believed God. It must have been a battle as he looked at his old body and Sarah's barrenness but faith rose within him as he hoped in the promise of God.

> *Against all hope, Abraham in hope believed and so became the father of many nations, just as it had been said to him, "So shall your offspring be."*
>
> Romans 4:18

His hope was rooted in God's character and promise. This is important. For our hope not to be presumption it must rest in who God is and what He has said.

There are four different types of hope

False hope: This is really no hope as it not only denies the facts but also the truth.

Forlorn hope: Which we have already referred to. This is hoping for a one in a million or billion chance.

Fanciful hope: This is plain old hype, trying to build something without foundations. It is destined to fail.

Faith filled hope: This is what the Bible speaks of because it is not trying to have faith in our faith but faith in the promises and power of God.

Whatever you are confronting, however big, dark or painful it may be, declare God's faithfulness over it and in the midst of it. As you do so the first change that happens will be in you. Instead of heaviness and fear, there will come peace and faith because the power of hope is being released.

God, who has so faithfully taken care of you in the past and is so faithfully taking care of you in the present, will also take care of you in the future.

Ask Him to fill you with His hope,

May the God of hope fill you with all joy and peace in believing, so that by the power of the Holy Spirit, you may abound in hope.

Romans 15:13

From Dying to Flying

God is the only one who can make
the valley of trouble a door of hope.

Catherine Marshall

From Dying to Flying

God Will Make A Way

A young child was asked by his mother what he had learned in Sunday school. "Well, Mum," he replied, "Our teacher told us how God sent Moses behind enemy lines on a rescue mission to lead the Israelites out of Egypt. When he got to the Red Sea, he had his engineers build a pontoon bridge and all the people walked across safely. Then he used his walkie-talkie to radio headquarters for reinforcements. They sent bombers to blow up the bridge and all the Israelites were saved." "Now, son, is that really what your teacher taught you?" his mother asked. "Well, no, Mum. But if I told it the way the teacher did, you'd never believe it!"

The story of the Israelites crossing the Red Sea is the miracle most referred to throughout the Old Testament. Yet what is so amazing is not only how God parted the water but why He led them there in the first place. It was an impossible situation. They were trapped. They could not go back because they were being pursued by Pharaoh's army who were out for bloody revenge, many of the soldiers had lost their firstborn sons and they were ready for a massacre.

The Promised Land was northeast of Egypt. So what did God do? He led them south. The reason we are told He did this was for them not to go through the land of the Philistines because they might change their minds and return to Egypt if they experienced war, (Exodus 13:17-18). So began the long march south by way of the wilderness towards the Red Sea. During this time a pattern emerged that would sadly last for the next forty years. The people complained and grumbled and God was compassionate and gracious.

When the Israelites arrived on the banks of the Red Sea it seemed there was no way back, or forward. Not only that, there were impassible mountain ranges and military fortresses to the west and east. Have you ever felt God has led you into an impossible place? Maybe that's where you are today. You have left Egypt and the initial thrill was amazing and even though the travel has been hot and dry the Lord has provided and protected. But now it seems there is no place to go. Confused and fearful we even wonder if it would have been better if we hadn't started the journey. What am I doing in the ministry? Why did I agree to get involved? Why isn't God answering my prayers? How did I end up here? What's going on with my health? We have come to our own Red Sea with the impending enemy behind us and impassible waters before us. Grief, anger, fear, bewilderment and hopelessness are just a few of the emotions we battle with. Yet God has not forsaken us, He is still in charge and always has been. This day the Israelites were going to cross over and the world's most fearsome army would never be a threat to them again.

In his book *A Dangerous Grace*, Charles Colson comments on some scientific research regarding the miracle of the Israelites crossing the Red Sea on dry ground. He says, "It is a well known scientific fact that a steady wind blowing over a body of water can change the water level. So two oceanographers decided to see if the same thing could happen on the narrow sliver of the Red Sea reaching up into the Gulf of Suez where, many scholars believe, the Israelites crossed as they were escaping from Pharaoh's army."

Writing in the *Bulletin of the American Meteorological Society,* the scientists concluded that a moderate wind blowing constantly for about ten hours (the time given in the Bible) could very well have caused the sea to recede a mile or two. The water level would drop ten feet, leaving dry land for the Israelites to cross. Later, an abrupt change in the wind would cause the water to return rapidly in a devastating wave. "The Gulf of Suez provides an ideal body of water for such a process because of its unique geography," said one of the scientists.

Colson observes, "The study does not prove the crossing happened this way, it shows that it was quite possible to do so. The skeptic might then argue that since there is a reasonably good natural explanation, then it wasn't a miracle after all. But if it was only a natural event, isn't it strange that God brought them to this exact spot, the waters only went back when Moses raised his staff and then came back again when he lowered it and drowned the Egyptians."

I have always enjoyed the story of the "liberal" preacher who told his congregation that miracles are only a figment of our enthusiasm and chance. He sought to illustrate his point by trying to prove that the Israelites crossing the Red Sea on dry ground was entirely false. He said they actually crossed over at another place called the Reed Sea which at that time of year had only a few inches of water. An elderly lady shouted out "Praise God, what a miracle!" The preacher responded, "You don't understand there was hardly any water." She said, "Yes I do, if what you are saying is right God managed to drown all those Egyptians in only a few inches of water!"

God Will Make a Way Where There Seems to be No Way, is a well known song by Don Moen. He relates the following story of tragedy and death, which led to him writing it. His sister-in-law, Susan Phelps, and her husband Craig, were involved in a car accident during a skiing trip travelling from their Oklahoma home to a resort in Colorado. While driving through Texas their van was hit by an eighteen wheeler lorry. A rear panel of their van was hit with such force that all four of the Phelps' children were thrown out.

In the darkness they were able to locate all of their injured children by their crying – all except one. Craig, who is a physician, finally located him beside a nearby fence. He was already dead. His neck had been broken.

As Craig picked up his son and tried to revive him, God said to him, "Jeremy is with me. You deal with those who are living." They sat for forty-five minutes out in the wilderness waiting for an ambulance.

Don was awakened in the middle of the night, his mother-in-law called to tell him of the tragic car accident involving his wife's sister, Susan. As Don and his wife grieved and poured out their hearts to the Lord, they felt helpless at communicating hope and grace to Susan and Craig.

While travelling by plane to Oklahoma, he began to read in Isaiah 43 where God says, *"I will even make a way in the wilderness and rivers in the desert."* He picked up his note pad and sketched a song that the Lord was giving him, he had been asked to sing at the memorial service. When he arrived he found that the Phelps had already selected Henry Smith's song, *Give Thanks*, for him to sing.

After the funeral Don, while holding Susan and Craig in his arms, said, "The Lord gave me a song for you," and he began to sing *God Will Make a Way, Where There Seems to be No Way*. He later made a taped copy of the song for Susan to play on her small cassette player just above her kitchen sink. He knew that when all the people had gone, and everything was said and done, that there would be days when she needed to hear that God was working in ways that she couldn't see.

Don continued, "About two years later I was called to sing in a small church in Dothan, Alabama. Although I had never intended to sing *God Will Make a Way* in a public service – I had written it just for that grieving family – somehow I felt impressed of the Lord to share the song with those people. I did so, and it had a tremendous impact on them."

> *God will make a way*
> *Where there seems to be no way*
> *He works in ways we cannot see*
> *He will make a way for me*
> *He will be my guide*
> *Hold me closely to His side*
> *With love and strength*
> *For each new day*
> *He will make a way*
> *He will make a way*

We live in a fallen world where bad things happen to good people. Our world and life are not always fair. Something has gone terribly wrong and sin has distorted everything. It will not be put right until Jesus returns.

To overcome and deal with this unfairness God offers us grace – grace that says even though it's not fair what you have gone through or are experiencing He is able to comfort, heal and restore for His grace is sufficient for you.

This amazing grace is not fair either. It's not fair that Jesus suffered in our place and took our punishment. It's not fair that the only scarred body in eternity will belong to Him. God's grace is greater than human fairness.

One of the most beautiful promises in the Old Testament was given by the prophet Hosea,

> *There I will give her back her vineyards, and*
> *will make the Valley of Achor a door of hope.*

Hosea 2:15

The Valley of Achor was a place of heartache and defeat. It's where Achan and his family were punished because his greed in coveting the silver and gold of Jericho led to Israel's defeat at Ai. You can read the tragic details in Joshua 7. The place became synonymous with things gone terribly wrong, but God says even there He will bless and transform the situation.

> What the enemy meant as a desert of despair
> God can make into a door of hope.

***The very things that held ya
down are gonna carry ya up,
and up, and up!***

Timothy Q Mouse
(Disney film – *Dumbo*)

From Dying to Flying

From Dying to Flying

The title for this book came one day as I was watching a documentary on Base Jumping. If you haven't got a clue what that is don't worry, I didn't know much about it either but this programme was very enlightening. It's when a climber carries a parachute or flying suit up to some high place on a mountain or other platform and instead of climbing back down they jump off and glide to the bottom.

It's not something I have a desire to do but I enjoy watching those who do and finding out why they do it. One of the reasons I have little inclination to try it out is because on two occasions while on holiday in Turkey at a resort famous for paragliding, my wife and I witnessed someone's equipment fail at around 2000 feet and they had to deploy their emergency parachute. Thankfully, they just about managed to land safely but any lingering ambitions I may have had to experience the thrill were "removed"! It was enough of an adrenalin rush watching them struggle coming down.

In the documentary there was an interview with one of the world's most famous "base jumpers" who described the elation involved in flying through the air. But it was something else he referred to that captured my attention. He said that climbing high peaks can be very dangerous and there are times when you reach out for a hand or foot hold and you are not sure if you will make it. On a few occasions he did this and either slipped or the rock gave way causing him to fall from the cliff and be hurtling thousands of feet to certain death. But after a few seconds he pulled the ripcord to the parachute on his back and there was the glorious sound of it opening and filling with air. His comment was, "There is no experience like it. One moment you are dying and the next you are flying. It is going from the worst possible experience to the best in just a few moments of time."

God has given us something far better than a "chute" on our back – we have the promise and presence of His amazing love and faithfulness.

Hopelessness is one of the worst experiences in life. It's like falling from a great height and waiting for the inevitable crash. On the way down dread and foreboding can become so awful you are almost glad when the bottom comes to get it over with. Such despair plays tricks with the mind. It doesn't even matter if you are really falling – so long as you think you are, or believe it will be bad news from the doctor or you will lose your job or a thousand other fearful possibilities – life is sucked out of you.

Hope means to trust that God's future is for us. It is knowing that He is in control not only of world history but our personal history. Whatever we face we do it with Him. Our future does not belong to chance or life's uncertainties – it belongs to God. He not only gives us hope for the future but hope and a future, Jeremiah 29:15.

Here's an interesting bit of trivia for you. Of all the songs ever written, which one do you think has been recorded the most by different vocal artists?

The answer is *Amazing Grace* written by John Newton in 1773 and it has been called the most famous hymn in history.

Before his conversion Newton lived a terrible life and been the captain of a slave ship. He was known as the "great blasphemer" and described himself as the greatest blasphemer on the high seas. He had a remarkable transformation after giving his life to Christ and another of his famous hymns begins, "How Sweet the Name of Jesus Sounds." But he is best known for *Amazing Grace* which he composed for his New Year's service at Olney, Northamptonshire, England. It was based on that morning's sermon text 1 Chronicles 17:16- 17, *"Then King David went in and sat before the Lord, and he said: 'Who am I, O Lord God, and what is my family, that you have brought me this far?'"*

The original title Newton gave to the song was not *Amazing Grace,* that was added much later, but *Faith's Review And Expectation.* God's grace that had saved him would keep him. It is full of thanks for what God had done and filled with hope for whatever may be ahead.

> *Thro' many dangers, toils and snares,*
> *I have already come;*
> *Tis grace has brought me safe thus far,*
> *And grace will lead me home.*

One of the verses Newton wrote that we do not often sing with the hymn is,

> *The Lord has promis'd good to*
> *me, His word my **hope** secures;*

From Dying to Flying

He will my shield and portion
be, As long as life endures.

Almost a hundred years before Newton penned his great hymn another famous preacher wrote his famous book *Pilgrim's Progress* in 1678. John Bunyan gave us not only a classic of English literature but a spiritual masterpiece of the trials and triumphs of the Christian life. More than 300 years after it was first published the book is still a best seller and has been translated into more than 200 languages. Not bad for someone with little formal education who went on to write over 50 other books. Although the exact timing is disputed Bunyan wrote the story of Pilgrim while in Bedford jail, imprisoned for twelve years for the crime of preaching without a licence. During this period he refused to bow to the dictatorial religious authorities and spent his time writing, praying, preaching to his fellow prisoners – a congregation of about sixty – and making shoelaces in his cell to help support his family. While imprisoned his only possessions were two books, John Foxe's *Book of Martyrs* and the Bible, a violin he had made out of tin, a flute he made from a chair leg, a supply of pen and paper and an abundance of God's grace and hope.

In the story of Pilgrim's journey to the Celestial City, he is joined on the final part by Hopeful. Along a rough stretch of road, Christian and Hopeful leave the highway to travel on the easier By -Path Meadow, where a rainstorm forces them to spend the night. In the morning they are captured by Giant Despair, who takes them to his Doubting Castle, where they are imprisoned, beaten and starved. The giant wants them to commit suicide, but they endure the ordeal until Christian realizes that a key he has, called Promise, will open all the doors and gates of Doubting Castle. Using the key, they escape.

Finally, after seeing the wonders of "Immanuel's Land" they stand on Mount Clear and are able to see the Celestial City. They make their way through the dangerous Enchanted Ground into the Land of Beulah, where they ready themselves to cross the River of Death to Mount Zion and the Celestial City. Christian has a rough time of it and it is Hopeful who helps him over, into the city.

Thank God for Hopeful.

Thank God for all those who bring hope into our lives.

Thank God for the power of hope that sets us free from the dungeons in the Castle of Giant Despair and helps us into the Celestial City.

Recently a good friend of mine phoned me from New Zealand. He is one of those wonderful people whose life and faith are contagious. I am sure if he were any happier he would be twins. However, the last several years have not been easy for him. He has battled with throat cancer, depression, bereavement and too many other things to mention but his trust and joy in God are infectious. He was told he would probably die but God restored his health. He is now putting on weight and at 65 said he feels and looks better than he has done for a long time. He has no plans of retiring and like Caleb is reminding God of all the promises He made to him.

Before his brush with death my friend led one of the fastest growing churches in New Zealand. Today, while no longer pastoring that fellowship, his passion for God and his work is undiminished.

He is writing books, discipling a wonderful group of people and filled with hope and excitement for the future. He is enjoying ministry more than he has ever done. There was a time when he felt he was dying not just physically but emotionally and spiritually, yet even in his darkest moments he knew God was carrying him and His promises were sure. Today he is flying again and so excited about the future because he knew how to pull the rip cord of hope on God's grace and power.

It is not always easy to hope, especially during what the Puritans called "the dark night of the soul." Those times that begin when you wonder where God is, and then it gets darker and you think, does God care? And it gets even bleaker and you begin to wonder whether there is a God. You still believe in the theological and historical God, but like the Psalmist your longing is to encounter the Living God, Psalm 42:2, 84:2. I wish I could be more like Job in those seasons, and sometimes I am, but at others I am more like Elijah sitting under the juniper tree or Thomas who says, "I have to see Jesus to believe!" It can be a battle. I am convinced that one of the devil's most deadly weapons is discouragement.

One of the strangest stories in the Bible is Elijah running away from Jezebel's threats, 1 Kings 19. If there was anyone who you thought would stand his ground it would be this fiery prophet. Hours before he had stood like a spiritual giant on Mount Carmel taunting the false prophets of Baal and calling fire down from heaven. He had spent his life standing up to Jezebel and her wimpy husband, Ahab, who was king. But now he was tired, emotionally and physically, and probably discouraged that there had not been a great turning to God in the nation as he expected after his mountain top experience. The demon queen threatened to kill him and we read this fearless man of God was afraid and ran for his life into the desert. Now, even more exhausted, he sat down under some shade and wanted his life to end. "I have had enough," he is saying, "No more it's over. I'm tired of praying, weary from hoping, exhausted from hiding." I often wonder how many times those words have been echoed by God's servants? The answer is too many to list, but here are just a few,

David:

> How long, O Lord? Will you forget me forever? How long will you hide your face from me? How long must I wrestle with my thoughts and every day have sorrow in my heart? How long will my enemy triumph over me?
>
> Psalm 13:1,2

But David knew how to encourage himself in God,

> But now, Lord, what do I look for? My **hope** is in you.
>
> Psalm 39:7

> Find rest, O my soul, in God alone; my **hope** comes from him.
>
> Psalm 62:5

Peter:

> I'm going fishing.
>
> John 21:3

I am indebted to the insights of New Testament and Greek scholar Kenneth Wuest in his *Word Studies*. He says, the words, "I'm going" are the translation of the Greek word *"hupago"* which mean, "this is the end, it's over, time for separate ways." It was Peter's formal announcement that he had had enough

It's his way of saying, "I'm going back to the family business and what I know best."

But this was not the end of the journey for Peter. Six weeks later he would say to a 40-year- old man who had never walked, *"Silver and gold I do not have, but such as I have I give to you, in the name of Jesus Christ of Nazareth, walk,"* Acts 3:6. And the man walked and ran and jumped and praised God!

A man without hope for his future will always go back to his past, but we must not allow our worst experiences to define our lives.

John Wesley:

There were times when he felt all spiritual life depart. In those times he would write to one person only and in code, to his beloved brother Charles. The code has long been broken so listen to what one of these letters read,

> "I do not feel the wrath of God abiding on me nor can I believe it does, but this is the mystery, I seem never to have loved God, therefore I never did, therefore I am only an honest heathen, a proselyte of the Temple. Yet to be so employed of God and to be so edged in I cannot go forward or backward. Surely there was never such an instance from the beginning of the world. I have no direct witness; I cannot even say that I am a child of God."

Yet at 88 years of age he was still preaching and his last words on this earth were, "The best of all God is with us."

Coming back to Elijah he was renewed and restored at a place called Horeb (interestingly it means devastation), often at our lowest point we experience God's amazing presence. When you read the passage (1 Kings 20), it sounds a little strange as the same wording repeats itself, but the meaning becomes clear when you understand that first Elijah heard the word of the Lord, and the second time he encountered the Lord of the word. Elijah came to understand that God isn't always in the fire or the earthquake, but sometimes in a still small voice. He is at work even when we do not realise it and He is sovereign, for it was not Jezebel or Ahab in control but Jehovah, and there were several thousand in the land that He had preserved who had not bowed their knee to idolatry.

Elijah had believed the demonic queen's lie that she would kill herself if she didn't destroy him, now he is set free and empowered with God's truth. He was not going to leave this world in Jezebel's coffin but Jehovah's chariot.

Soar Like The Eagle

Several hundred years later the Prophet Isaiah was comforting God's people who had been taken into exile. Their home and everything that made life worth living had been taken from them. Isaiah 40 begins, *"Comfort, comfort my people,"* and they are reminded of God's greatness and His care for them. Everything else may have changed for them but He had not. The last few verses of that chapter are some of the best known in the whole of the Old Testament,

> *He gives strength to the weary and increases the power of the weak. Even youths grow tired and weary, and young men stumble and fall;*

*but those who **hope** in the Lord will renew
their strength. They will soar on wings like
eagles; they will run and not grow weary, they
will walk and not be faint.*

Isaiah 40:29-31

Many are familiar with the words *"Those who wait upon the
Lord."* But the Hebrew word translated wait is *Qavah* which
implies "waiting with hope and expectation." Isaiah tells them
that as they do this the power of God is released within them.
Instead of struggling to survive, they will soar like eagles.

If our revelation of God is not greater than our circumstances we
will always be controlled by them – we will live under not above
them. Throughout Isaiah 40 the prophet wants the people to turn
their eyes and their faith to God and off their desperate
circumstances. This is how we ride the wind of God.

The eagle's majestic flight is powerfully described by Jamie
Buckingham in his book *Where Eagles Soar.* While on a trip to
the Sinai Peninsula, his party had reached the summit of Mount
Sinai and it was there they spotted the eagle. A huge storm had
built up over the Gulf of Suez and was moving inland while the
mighty thunderclouds towered around 30,000 feet – it was
awesome to behold. But it was the eagle flying which drew their
attention.

> "Watch the eagle," said our Israeli guide
> pointing high above the Sinai desert at the
> silent figure soaring close to the mountains.
> "He locks his wings, picks the thermals and
> rides the breath of God above the storm, that's
> what the prophet meant when he said we
> would soar like eagles." "How high will he go,"
> I asked?

"Over the storm," said our guide, "25,000, 30,000 feet. He is now beyond his own control, he locks his wings at his shoulders and rides the wind of God. He fears nothing and even though we can no longer see him he can see us – he can see for 50 miles. He will go so high he will be covered with ice, his head, his wings, everything. Then he descends on the backside of the storm and the ice melts. Who knows if it were not for the ice he might just keep going up, touch God and never come down."

From eagles to elephants – one of my favourite Disney films is *Dumbo,* which tells the story of the baby elephant whose ears are so big everyone makes fun of him. His mother works in a circus and loves him very much and is very protective of him. There is also a mouse named Timothy Q, who befriends the sad and frightened Dumbo. One night they end up getting drunk and the next morning waking up in a tree!

Timothy Q starts wondering how they managed to end up in a tree.

"Now I wonder how we ever got up in that tree, anyway? Now, let's see – elephants can't climb trees, can they? Nah, nah, that's ridiculous. Would they jump up? Mm-mmm. Too high." (A crow shouts, 'Hey there, son. Maybe y'all flew up.')

The mouse realises that's what must have happened. He says, "That's it! Dumbo! You flew! Boy, am I stupid. Why didn't I think of this before? Your ears! Just look at 'em, Dumbo! Why, they're perfect wings! The very things that held ya down are gonna carry ya up, and up, and up!"

Dumbo and the mouse go back to the circus and perform. As part of his act Dumbo has to jump from a great height and on his way crashing to the ground his massive ears unflap and he glides through the air as everyone applauds and is amazed. He winds up the star of the show and is reunited with his mother. The little elephant with the big ears went from dying to flying.

That's one of the amazing things about God. He can take the very things that are "holding us down" to lift us up. Our greatest tests can become our greatest testimonies and the biggest mess can become our most powerful message when God redeems it.

But in your hearts set apart Christ as Lord. Always be prepared to give an answer to everyone who asks you to give the reason for the hope that you have.

1 Peter 3:15

From Dying to Flying

Reasons to Hope

On July 19, 64 AD, there was a great fire that destroyed much of Rome and its citizens angrily looked for someone to blame for the catastrophe. We now know it was the mad Emperor Nero who had started it because he wanted to pull down parts of the city for his great building projects. But when he saw the fury of the mob he quickly shifted blame onto the newly formed groups of Christians and so began one of the greatest persecutions of the Early Church.

Terrible atrocities took place and when news of this barbarism spread through the empire fear and terror went with it. It is into this situation that Peter wrote to prepare believers for the trials they would endure. Peter himself would eventually die in that period, crucified in Rome. But his letters are full of hope because Jesus has conquered death and is coming again.

Jesus' Resurrection

> *Praise be to the God and Father of our Lord Jesus Christ! In his great mercy he has given us new birth into a **living hope** through the resurrection of Jesus Christ from the dead.*

> 1 Peter 1:3

The two disciples on the Emmaus Road (Luke 24) were men who were giving up because they had lost hope. They were walking to Emmaus but in reality they were running from Jerusalem. It had been a horrific weekend. Jesus had been hung on a cross and laid in a tomb and all their dreams and longings of who He was and what He would do had been crucified and buried with Him.

Jesus had just accomplished the most important event in history, something planned before the world was made. Through the cross and resurrection He had secured the greatest victory over satan. His shed blood opened the way to approach God. The curtain in the Temple was torn from top to bottom and dead saints were seen alive again in Jerusalem.

In the midst of all these immense events Jesus took time for an unhurried walk with two discouraged and disillusioned disciples, which shows the amazing lengths to which Jesus goes to help hurting saints. He drew alongside and His questions opened the gates of the grief in their hearts so all the pent up disappointment came pouring out.

At first they didn't recognise it was Jesus. Why should they? He was the last person they expected to see and we read they were kept from doing so. He asked them why they looked so sad and they revealed the source of their heartache. They had been discussing what had happened,

> *But we had **hoped** that he was the one who was going to redeem Israel.*
>
> Luke 24:21

"We had hoped." These words reveal their deep pain and shattered hope. Even when the women returned from the tomb and told them it was empty and Jesus was alive it made no difference. Neither did the testimony of the other disciples who confirmed what the women had said.

So, lovingly and patiently, Jesus revealed God's plan and purposes to these two unnamed men and their hearts began to "burn" again. Their emotions were not only being stirred but healing was taking place in His presence through His Word. When they broke bread together at the end of the day they saw who He was. They began that day faces downcast escaping from Jerusalem to Emmaus, but ended it running back to Jerusalem, shouting, *"It is true! The Lord has risen!"* (Luke 24:34.)

The resurrection changes everything!

A few years ago my father died suddenly of heart failure. He was seventy three years of age and in relatively good health. He had just taken my mother to a ladies prayer meeting at their church and went to a supermarket nearby. While sitting in the car outside his heart failed and he passed into the presence of the Lord. It was sudden and unexpected, but he had already made his peace with God many years before and when his time came all my father had to do was die. Because he had a living faith death held no fears.

When I spoke at his funeral service I told everyone of his journey to faith in Christ. When he was in his thirties he had a serious accident while working as a coal miner and spent a whole year in hospital after being told he would never walk again. During that time the local Baptist pastor came to visit him and although my dad was not a religious man he promised that when he came home he would bring his wife and children to church. Amazingly, many months later he walked out of the hospital and after a few weeks sought to keep his promise. The first Sunday he went to church alone and parked his car outside the building listening to the singing, but he could not bring himself to go inside. There was a battle going on within him. A few weeks later he tried again and this time went inside, and for the next several years as a family we attended church regularly. Sadly, we drifted from the church but years later my mum and dad were invited to a Pentecostal church where they immediately felt at home. For the next thirty years they attended and served faithfully. I remember vividly the thrill of seeing my dad lift those huge coal miners' hands in praise and worship. Something truly wonderful had happened in his life since he met Jesus.

My opening remarks at the service were, "*'We grieve today but not as those without hope,'* (1Thessalonians 4:13). My dad knew and loved Jesus so we can say with confidence, *'To be absent from the body is to be present with the Lord,'* (2Corinthians 5:8)."

Here is part of the message I gave that day,

> Where do I begin? I have lost a dad and a great friend. We have lost so much but in another sense we haven't lost him at all because we know where he is. He always joked with me

that he wanted me to take his funeral service, he had a great sense of humour, and he wanted Jan (my wife) to play the organ as that way it would all be free.

A godly young man named Jim Elliot was martyred for his faith when just 29 years old. Years before he wrote in his journal, "He is no fool who gives what he cannot keep, to gain what he cannot lose." He had also written, "When your time comes to die, make sure that all you have to do is die." My father died suddenly but when his time came he was ready, all he had to do was die.

I concluded by saying, "Dad, we love you and miss you so much and thank God for the ways you touched and embraced our lives." I turned to his coffin covered in flowers beside me and said, "Dad, you are not in that coffin, you are with Jesus." I then addressed death and declared, "Death you have won no victory this day," and quoted the Apostle Paul's words,

> *Where, O death, is your victory? Where, O death, is your sting? The sting of death is sin, and the power of sin is the law. But thanks be to God! He gives us the victory through our Lord Jesus Christ.*
>
> 1 Corinthians 15:55-57

Jesus' Redemption

> *For you know that it was not with perishable things such as silver or gold that you were redeemed from the empty way of life handed down to you from your forefathers, but with the precious blood of Christ, a lamb without blemish or defect... Through him you believe in God, who raised him from the dead and glorified him, and so your faith and **hope** are in God.*
>
> 1 Peter 1:18-21

Note the words, *"redeemed from the empty way of life handed down by your forefathers."* Peter is addressing Jews who had come to believe in Jesus as the Messiah. They are told that all of their former religion without Christ was barren and empty. I love the Jewish people and believe God still has a special purpose for them, but they need Jesus' blood to wash and cleanse them the same way as any other pagan or gentile.

The blood in Scripture speaks not only of sacrifice and death but also of salvation and life, (Leviticus 17:11). Jesus not only gave His life for us by His death on the cross, but through His resurrection is able to give His life to us. Our hope therefore, is certain because Jesus does not change and His blood will never lose its power. When John Newton was on his death bed, his last words were to his good friend William Jay. He whispered, "My memory is nearly gone. But I remember two things: That I am a great sinner." He paused for breath. "And that Christ is a great saviour."

The Pit

There was a man who one day fell into a deep dark pit and cried out for help.

* A Buddhist came along and said, "You only think that you are in a pit."

* A Muslim came by and said, "Try to be good in your pit and one day you may get out."

* A Jehovah's Witness came by and asked, "Would you like to read my magazine? It has stories about a lot of other people in pits."

* A Mormon said, "You can be a god in your pit."

* An atheist came by and said, "I do not believe in pits."

* An agnostic walked past saying, "I'm not sure if that is a pit."

* An optimist said, "Things could have been worse."

* A pessimist said, "Things will get worse!"

* A tax inspector asked if he was paying taxes on the pit.

* A government official wanted to know if he had a permit for his pit.

* A lawyer, excited, asked if he had injured himself falling into the pit.

* A self pitying person said, "You haven't seen anything until you've seen my pit!"

* A Pharisee said, "Only bad people fall into a pit."

* A relativist said, "Each to their own pit."

Jesus, seeing the man, got down into the pit with him and carried him out, because no pit can hold Him.

He redeems my life from the pit

Psalm 103:4

"There is no pit so deep, that God's love is not deeper still."

Corrie Ten Boom

Jesus' Return

*Therefore, prepare your minds for action; be self-controlled; set your **hope** fully on the grace to be given you when Jesus Christ is revealed.*

1 Peter 1:13

Billy Graham tells us in his autobiography, *Just As I Am,* how in 1954 Winston Churchill asked to meet with him. Graham and his team had held months of highly successful meetings in London and the British Prime Minister wanted to know why so many came night after night to hear him preach. Graham told him that it was God's doing and that people were eager to hear from God. Churchill looked the American evangelist in the eye and said, "I am a man without hope – do you have any real hope?" Graham recounts, "He might have been talking geopolitically but to me this sounded like a personal plea and in notes I jotted down after the meeting I recalled he referred to hopelessness no fewer than nine times. His bouts with depression are now well documented although I was not aware of them at the time.

I asked him, 'Are you without hope for your own soul's salvation?' Frankly, Churchill replied, 'I think about that a great deal.'

"I had my New Testament with me, knowing we had only a few minutes left and I immediately explained the way of salvation. I watched carefully for signs of irritation or offence but he seemed receptive. I talked about God's plan for the future and return of Christ. His eyes seemed to lighten up at this prospect."

At precisely 12.30pm his secretary, Mr Colville, knocked the door and said, "Sir Winston, the Duke of Windsor is here for your luncheon." Church growled, "Let him wait," and waived Colville away and turning back to Billy Graham said, go ahead.

"I went on for a further 15 minutes then I asked if I could pray. 'Most certainly,' he said, standing up to appreciate it. I prayed for the difficult situations he faced every day as Prime Minister and acknowledged God was the only hope for the world and for us individually. Mr Churchill thanked me as we walked out."

That's not the only time Billy Graham tells about world leaders wanting to know about Jesus' return. Maybe it's because they know better than anyone that human power and governments are not able to solve this world's problems and bring about harmony and peace.

Graham speaks of the time he was with John F Kennedy being driven to the Kennedy's home. Suddenly, Kennedy, who was now President elect, turned to him and asked, "Do you believe in the Second Coming of Jesus Christ?" "I most certainly do," said Graham. "Does my church (Roman Catholic) believe it?" asked Kennedy. "They have it in their creeds," Graham responded. "But they don't preach it, they don't talk much about it," said the future president, "I'd like to know what you think." So Graham says he explained what the Bible said about Christ coming the first time, dying on a cross, rising from the dead and then promising He would come back again. "Only then, are we going to have permanent world peace," added Graham.

The Bible describes Jesus' second coming not only as being our hope but calls it a *blessed hope*, Titus 2:13. The Apostle John tells us that this hope has a purifying and cleansing effect, 1John 3:2,3. When the writers use the word "hope" they are not saying that it would be nice if it happened or they wish it was true. They are telling us that it is a joyful certainty.

There are almost two thousand references to Christ's second coming in the Old Testament and 318 references to it in the New Testament – an amazing one out of every 30 verses. For every prophecy in the Bible concerning Christ's first coming, there are eight which look forward to His second!

We don't know the exact timing of when this will happen, but we know the signs leading to it are described by Jesus to be like labour pains increasing in frequency and intensity as the day approaches, (Matthew 24:8). There was even an expectancy and longing for this in the early church when the power of the Gospel spread throughout the world as Jesus said must first happen before He returned, (Matthew 24:14).

During the Queen's coronation in 1953 the Archbishop of Canterbury, Dr Geoffrey Fisher, extended to Her Majesty the crown with these poignant words, "I give thee, O Sovereign Lady, this crown to wear until He who reserves the right to wear it shall return." Jesus is not only the only hope for the individual but also for the whole world.

The End of All and the Beginning of All

In his book *Journey of Desire,* John Eldridge talks about *The Great Restoration* when at the end of the age God will restore and renew all of His creation. It is a magnificent scene that is portrayed. Eldridge says,

> Most Christians have some idea of heaven and eternity as a never ending church service. (Doesn't the Bible say saints worship God in heaven?) An endless church service, our hearts sink, is that all it is?

Heaven is not about harps and halo's and endless hymns (or choruses if you are more charismatic). It is about the breathtaking glory and grandeur of being reunited with loved ones in Christ, of intimate fellowship with God and reigning and ruling a renewed earth and universe. We will explore the wonders of the cosmos as we enter into the joy of our master, (Matthew 25:21). We will also forever be discovering new wonders and facets about the God we worship and adore.

Eldridge goes on to quote Annie Dillard, in her book *Pilgrim at Tinker Creek*, where she recounts the stories that were reported of blind men and women who received some of the first cataract operations,

> A little girl visits a garden, she is greatly astonished, and can scarcely be persuaded to answer, stands speechless, in front of the tree, which she only names on taking hold of it... One girl was eager to tell her blind friend that men do not really look like trees at all, and was astounded to discover that her every visitor had an utterly different face. Finally, a twenty-two-year-old girl was dazzled by the

world's brightness and kept her eyes shut for two weeks. When, at the end of that time, she opened her eyes again, she did not recognize any objects but the more she now directed her gaze on everything about her, the more it could be seen how an expression of gratification and astonishment overspread her features, she repeatedly exclaimed, "Oh God, how beautiful!"

This old creation can be so breathtaking so what will it be like when restored to full glory and splendour? The old gospel song which says, "This world is not my home, I am just a – passing through, my treasures are laid up somewhere beyond the blue," is true in the sense that God has something much better in store. However, whereas this world is not our home this earth is going to be.

Peter does say this earth will be destroyed and writes some terrifying things about the end of the age, (2 Peter 3:12,) but the context is of this world being once destroyed by the flood, however the earth was not annihilated but remained, Genesis 6-7. It was cleansed of death and corruption and restored again. The word Peter used translated "destroyed" (2 Peter 3:10) has the meaning of being exposed to judgement, to be purified. Our fallen world with its misery and pain and our frail bodies subject to weakness and death will be transformed and renewed, Romans 8:19-25.

Revelation 21:5 *"I am making all things new,"* does not say "I am making all new things." It means that the things so badly damaged will be restored and made even better than they were. Paradise lost will be paradise restored. The New Jerusalem is not floating in the clouds but coming down from heaven to earth so that the dwelling of God will be with men.

> *Then I saw a new heaven and a new earth, for the first heaven and the first earth had passed away, and there was no longer any sea. I saw the Holy City, the New Jerusalem, coming down out of heaven from God, prepared as a bride beautifully dressed for her husband. And I heard a loud voice from the throne saying, "Now the dwelling of God is with men, and he will live with them. They will be his people, and God himself will be with them and be their God.*
>
> *"He will wipe every tear from their eyes. There will be no more death or mourning or crying or pain, for the old order of things has passed away."*
>
> Revelation 21:1-4

The theologian and philosopher Dallas Willard says in his book *The Divine Conspiracy,*

> The life we now have as the persons we now are will continue in the universe in which we now exist. The earth has been our home and will be our home in eternity.
>
> I meet many faithful Christians who in spite of their faith, are deeply disappointed in how their lives have turned out. Sometimes, it is simply a matter of how they experience ageing, which they take to mean they no longer have a future. But often, due to

circumstances or wrongful decisions and actions by others, what they had hoped to accomplish in life they did not... Much of the distress of these good people comes from a failure to realize that their life lies before them... The life that lies endlessly before us in the kingdom of God.

At the end of his book, *Just As I Am*, Billy Graham looks forward to the life to come,

No I don't know the future, but I do know this, the best is yet to be! Heaven awaits us, and that will be far, far more glorious than anything we can imagine.

I know that my life will soon be over. I thank God for it, and for all he has given me in this life. But I look forward to heaven. I look forward to the reunion with friends and loved ones who have gone on before. I look forward to heaven's freedoms from sorrow and pain. I also look forward to serving God in ways we can't begin to imagine.

This is what it means to have *"Christ in you, the hope of glory,"* Colossians 1:27.

Guide me in your truth and teach me,
for you are God my Saviour and
my hope is in you all day long.

Psalm 25:5

From Dying to Flying

Hope Again

I "hope" (trust and confidently expect) that this book will inspire you to grow in hope and if you have lost hope then to begin to hope again. I want to finish by sharing some amazing stories. The first one is about a very good friend of mine.

Dai Chopstix

Tony Nam, or Dai Chopstix as he likes to refer to himself, is a Chinese Welshman who my wife and I have come to love and admire dearly. Several years ago, he was diagnosed with a very aggressive cancer and radical surgery was required. The prognosis was not good but as he testifies below, God is incredibly good.

> In July 2008, a tumour was found in my bladder. On removal of the tumour, I was informed by the registrar (urology) that not all the cancer had been removed. It had already infiltrated the muscle and the wall of my bladder. Furthermore, unless I received radical radiotherapy or surgical removal of

my bladder within the next month or so, the cancer would break out of my bladder and spread throughout my body. On leaving the registrar's office, in agreement my wife Marian and I resolved... *we shall not come under the spirit of fear, our trust is in the Lord.*

When I chose removal of the bladder I was referred to the top consultant urologist in west Wales and a pre-operation interview arranged. At this interview the consultant's opening words were, "Mr Nam, you have an extremely nasty, aggressive cancer and your bladder must be removed as soon as possible together with your prostate and lymph glands..." The pros and cons of a neo-bladder or stoma bag were presented to me so that I could make an informed decision of which procedure should be followed when the operation was carried out. Before this interview was concluded, however, I said to the consultant I needed to say something to him. What I said was:

"I am a Christian. I believe, indeed know that Jesus is alive and heals today. I know that Jesus heals through the medical profession; I have no problem with that, as the Gospel writer Luke was a physician. But Jesus also heals through miracles. I have and will continue to receive a lot of powerful prayers and ministry for the removal of the cancer in my body. What I would hate to happen is, for you to remove the bladder, send it to the pathology laboratory for analysis and for the pathologist to say to you, 'why have you removed a perfectly healthy bladder?' So, is there anyway you can check me out before you put the knife in?"

The consultant agreed that he would examine the bladder internally with a camera and on opening me up, would further examine the bladder visually and by touch... and should he conclude that the bladder need not be removed, he would be doing this based on my faith and not his.

On the evening of Thursday, September 25, I was admitted to the hospital. On the Friday morning, the consultant's registrar asked me to sign the consent form for two procedures, an examination by camera following which they would remove my bladder etc. **"May remove my bladder,"** I responded, to which the registrar said that they expected to remove the bladder and were only inserting the camera for my peace of mind as I'd requested the consultant so to do. I said to the registrar that I had an expertise in my professional field just as they had an expertise in their professional field. I also presumed that they had a professional integrity such that they would do or not do whatever was correct, and so I had no problem with entrusting my body into their care.

I was wheeled into the anaesthetic room... and the next thing I remember was being in the recovery unit and the registrar saying,

"Mr Nam, we have not removed your bladder." To which I responded "Alleluia!" **He then said that they could see no sign of cancer in my bladder or in the tissue sample he removed from the site of the tumour.** All I could say was "Praise the Lord." And then went back to "sleep".

Unknown to me whilst I was asleep in the hospital and prior to the surgical team's investigations... my wife, Marian, was woken at 4am by a bright light in our bedroom and which she knew was a heavenly visitation. Whether it was Jesus, *the Light of the World,* or an angel... she doesn't know, but what she does know is that she was not shocked by this supernatural visitation, but felt such a peace and joy within her. Hardly the feelings one would normally expect knowing one's husband was in hospital to undergo major surgery.

Prior to my knowing that I had received a miraculous healing, Marian took a phone call from the consultant who told her *that he could not justify removing a perfectly healthy bladder.*

I was discharged early the following Sunday and my wife Marian, and I decided that we should not immediately go home, but first go to our church meeting to give thanks to the Lord for the miraculous healing I had received. When I arrived in the church, a microphone was put in my hand and I spoke as the Holy Spirit gave me the words, and here's what I said, here's what I believe this testimony is all about.

"The lesson God wants to give to the church, and that means you, through this miraculous healing is... you must be bolder in professing your faith...you must be bolder in professing what you believe... and not in an academic intellectual way, but in an active way, in the market place, in a relevant way. Think about it guys. If I had not had the audacity... not been so bold as to tell the consultant surgeon what I believed, I would not be here now giving this testimony. Instead, I would still be in the intensive care ward, and minus my bladder, prostate and lymph glands. Praise the Lord."

Since the above testimony was written two things have happened.

First, the histopathology report of the biopsy that was taken during the operation that never was has been received which stated, **"No tumour/transitional cell carcinoma is seen."** And, **"No dysplasia, residual or recurrent Transitional Cell Carcinoma or any other malignancy is seen."**

And secondly, in October 2008, for the peace of mind of the medical practitioners who were looking after me, I had an MRI scan, the report of which concluded, **"If multiple deep biopsies have revealed no tumour**

then perhaps a follow up study after a suitable interval (3 – 4 months) might be recommended to assess changes of these appearances having allowed for post operative changes to settle." Or in other words, as the high grade, aggressive, invasive cancer that was observed when the tumour was removed can no longer be found, it would be prudent to "kick for touch", and check it out again.

Then on May 2009, seven months after the MRI scan and ten months after the malignant tumour was removed, to satisfy the urologist, I allowed them to examine me once again with an internal camera and take further and more extensive samples from my bladder for a biopsy. The urologist is still perplexed, but announced that there was no sign, visually or on analysis of any tumour or malignancy.

I meet with and have contact with Tony and his wife regularly, and he is busy serving God and enjoying good health.

Praying for Conversion

George Muller, the great Victorian Christian and social reformer, tells a story of persistent prayer in his diary,

"In November 1844, I began to pray for the conversion of five individuals. I prayed every day without a single intermission, whether sick or in health, on the land, on the sea, and whatever the pressure of my engagements might be. Eighteen months elapsed before

the first of the five was converted. I thanked
God and prayed on for the others. Five years
elapsed, and then the second was converted. I
thanked God for the second, and prayed on
for the other three. Day by day, I continued to
pray for them, and six years passed before the
third was converted. I thanked God for the
three, and went on praying for the other two.
These two remained unconverted."

Thirty-six years later he wrote that the other two, sons of one of
Muller's friends, were still not converted. He wrote, "But I hope
in God, I pray on, and look for the answer. They are not converted
yet, but they will be." In 1897, fifty-two years after he began to
pray daily, without interruption, for these two men, they were
finally converted – but after he died!5

Does God Believe in Atheists?

Dr Luis Flores Olmedo was professor of pedagogy in the
Department of Philosophy of the Central University in Quito,
Ecuador. He had written five textbooks in the field of learning
theory and over 200 journalistic articles. His studies took him to
Europe, Egypt and the Soviet Union. He was also well known as
the author of a booklet – *How to Raise the Ideal Atheist Family.*
In the booklet he used his wife and four children as the model for
the godless family. Though he was not a member of the
communist party, he did hold the position of intellectual leader of
the campus Marxist movement. He took particular delight in
ridiculing the faith of anyone who might believe in God – Catholic
or evangelical protestant.

In May 1982, the Puerto Rican Pentecostal Yeye Avila held an
evangelistic campaign in Quito's bull ring. Flores' wife and his

oldest daughter Gabriela, were invited and decided to attend one of the meetings. Both women were physically healed at the meeting and as a result became Christians. Gabriela also spoke in tongues. The younger children also became Christians during the campaign despite their atheistic training.

> Shortly after his wife and four daughters' conversions, Dr Flores arrived home from the university to find his family on their knees praying for his conversion. When Gabriela saw her father entering the room she said, "Daddy, I am going to prove to you once and for all that there is a God and that Jesus Christ is alive today – I am going to sing for you in a language I have never learned."

> She then proceeded to sing as the Holy Spirit gave her the words. She sang in Russian, then German, then Italian, then French and finally English. It was music that exalted the Lord and was sung to a well known tune *La Tabacundena*, written by the professor some years before. Dr Flores was familiar with each language and knew his daughter did not know them – the experience left him shaken.

> He did not sleep that night. The next morning he cancelled all his classes and locked himself inside his office, because of the presence of a power he was unable to deal with.

> That evening he returned home to find his family praying for him again. Gabriela again approached him and this time laid hands on

him and prophesied over him revealing specific sins in his life.

He had had enough – he dropped to his knees saying, "Lord, I am a fool," and offering his life to God. At that time Dr Flores recalls God picked him up off the floor and shook him like a doll, three times. In the process he was healed of a displaced lumbar vertebra, haemorrhoids and numerous allergies and he also spoke in tongues.

On March 14, 1989, he was ordained. Today Flores is pastor of Centro Christiano Vida Abundate (Abundant Christian Life Centre) where he leads a rapidly growing church. He also oversees outreach to the Quicha Indians living in remote districts of Ecuador.6

5 *Deepening Your Conversation With God* by Ben Patterson C 1999 Bethany House Publishers, p 105-106

6 John Wimber *Power Evangelism* p 115-117. Conversation drawn from interviews with Jerry Brown, an AOG missionary from Ecuador and a close friend of Dr Flores. Conducted at Fuller Theological, California in Feb 1991.

From Dying to Flying

Prayer:

Heavenly Father, thank you for your great faithfulness. In the darkness you have been my light. In the storm you have been my anchor. In every trial you have been my peace. In every battle you have been my strength and my deliverer. You have promised to never leave me nor forsake me and as I recall all you have done in my past I trust you completely for the future as I rest now in the present.

I ask you to fill me with an infusion of hope. I confess in faith something good is going to happen in my life as I trust in you. I look to you as the source of my healing, provision and deliverance. I thank you for your faithfulness in the past and that you have already taken care of the future.

From Dying to Flying

But as for me, I watch in hope for the Lord, I wait for God my Saviour; my God will hear me.

Micah 7:7

Other books by
David Holdaway

The Life of Jesus
The Life of Jesus More Than A prophet
Never Enough
Money and Spiritual Warfare
Surviving and Succeeding in a Financial Crisis
Was Jesus Rich?
How to Stand Against a Spiritual Attack
No More Fear
Winning Over Worry
Revival is a Heart Issue
Footholds and Strongholds
The Wonder of Christmas
Jesus The Wonder of Christmas
The Captured Heart
The Burning Heart
Issues of the Heart
What Word do all University Professors Spell
Wrong?
They Saw Jesus

All these books are available in good book
shops and also by contacting the author

Davidholdaway1@aol.com
www.davidholdaway.org.uk
Tel. (00 44) (0) 1685 374675

From Dying to Flying

From Dying to Flying